A Child's Garden of Verses

A Child's Garden of Verses

Robert Louis Stevenson

Illustrated by Diane Goode

Afterword by Peter Glassman

BOOKS OF WONDER
WILLIAM MORROW AND COMPANY
NEW YORK

For Peter

—D.G.

Illustrations copyright © 1998 by Diane Goode
Afterword copyright © 1998 by Peter Glassman

Published by William Morrow and Company, Inc.
1350 Avenue of the Americas, New York, NY 10019
www.williammorrow.com
Books of Wonder
16 West Eighteenth Street, New York, NY 10011

Printed in the United States of America.

1 3 5 7 9 10 8 6 4 2

Library of Congress Cataloging-in-Publication Data
Stevenson, Robert Louis, 1850–1894.
A child's garden of verses / Robert Louis Stevenson;
illustrated by Diane Goode; afterword by Peter Glassman.
p. cm. — (Books of wonder)
Summary: A collection of poems evoking
the world and feelings of childhood.
ISBN 0-688-14584-1
1. Children's poetry, Scottish. [1. Scottish poetry.]
I. Goode, Diane, ill. II. Title. III. Series.
PR5489.C5 1998 821'.8—dc21 97-32913 CIP AC

Books of Wonder is a registered trademark of Ozma, Inc.

TO ALISON CUNNINGHAM
From Her Boy

For the long nights you lay awake
And watched for my unworthy sake:
For your most comfortable hand
That led me through the uneven land:
For all the storybooks you read:
For all the pains you comforted:

For all you pitied, all you bore,
In sad and happy days of yore—
My second mother, my first wife,
The angel of my infant life—
From the sick child, now well and old,
Take, nurse, the little book you hold!

And grant it, Heaven, that all who read
May find as dear a nurse at need,
And every child who lists my rhyme,
In the bright, fireside, nursery clime,
May hear it in as kind a voice
As made my childish days rejoice!

R.L.S.

Contents

THE CHILD ALONE

A Child's
Garden of Verses

BED IN SUMMER

In winter I get up at night
And dress by yellow candlelight.
In summer, quite the other way,
I have to go to bed by day.

I have to go to bed and see
The birds still hopping on the tree,
Or hear the grown-up people's feet
Still going past me in the street.

And does it not seem hard to you,
When all the sky is clear and blue,
And I should like so much to play,
To have to go to bed by day?

A THOUGHT

It is very nice to think
The world is full of meat and drink,
With little children saying grace
In every Christian kind of place.

At the Seaside

When I was down beside the sea
A wooden spade they gave to me
To dig the sandy shore.

My holes were empty like a cup.
In every hole the sea came up,
Till it could come no more.

YOUNG NIGHT-THOUGHT

All night long and every night,
When my mama puts out the light,
I see the people marching by,
As plain as day, before my eye.

Armies and emperors and kings,
All carrying different kinds of things,
And marching in so grand a way,
You never saw the like by day.

So fine a show was never seen
At the great circus on the green;
For every kind of beast and man
Is marching in that caravan.

At first they move a little slow,
But still the faster on they go,
And still beside them close I keep
Until we reach the town of Sleep.

WHOLE DUTY OF CHILDREN

A child should always say what's true
And speak when he is spoken to,
And behave mannerly at table;
At least as far as he is able.

RAIN

The rain is raining all around,
It falls on field and tree,
It rains on the umbrellas here,
And on the ships at sea.

PIRATE STORY

Three of us afloat in the meadow by the swing,
  Three of us aboard in the basket on the lea.
Winds are in the air, they are blowing in the spring,
  And waves are on the meadow like the waves there are at sea.

Where shall we adventure, today that we're afloat,
  Wary of the weather and steering by a star?
Shall it be to Africa, a-steering of the boat,
  To Providence, or Babylon, or off to Malabar?

Hi! But here's a squadron a-rowing on the sea—
  Cattle on the meadow a-charging with a roar!
Quick, and we'll escape them, they're as mad as they can be,
  The wicket is the harbor and the garden is the shore.

THE SUN TRAVELS

The sun is not abed, when I
At night upon my pillow lie;
Still round the earth his way he takes,
And morning after morning makes.

While here at home, in shining day,
We round the sunny garden play,
Each little Indian sleepyhead
Is being kissed and put to bed.

And when at eve I rise from tea,
Day dawns beyond the Atlantic Sea;
And all the children in the West
Are getting up and being dressed.

WINDY NIGHTS

Whenever the moon and stars are set,
   Whenever the wind is high,
All night long in the dark and wet,
   A man goes riding by.
Late in the night when the fires are out,
Why does he gallop and gallop about?

Whenever the trees are crying aloud,
   And ships are tossed at sea,
By, on the highway, low and loud,
   By at the gallop goes he.
By at the gallop he goes, and then
By he comes back at the gallop again.

TRAVEL

I should like to rise and go
Where the golden apples grow —
Where below another sky
Parrot islands anchored lie,
And, watched by cockatoos and goats,
Lonely Crusoes building boats —
Where in sunshine reaching out
Eastern cities, miles about,
Are with mosque and minaret
Among sandy gardens set,
And the rich goods from near and far
Hang for sale in the bazaar —
Where the Great Wall round China goes,
And on one side the desert blows,
And with bell and voice and drum,
Cities on the other hum —
Where are forests, hot as fire,
Wide as England, tall as a spire,
Full of apes and coconuts
And the Negro hunters' huts —

Where the knotty crocodile
Lies and blinks in the Nile,
And the red flamingo flies
Hunting fish before his eyes—
Where in jungles, near and far,
Man-devouring tigers are,
Lying close and giving ear
Lest the hunt be drawing near,
Or a comer-by be seen
Swinging in a palanquin—
Where among the desert sands
Some deserted city stands,
All its children, sweep and prince,
Grown to manhood ages since,
Not a foot in street or house,
Not a stir of child or mouse,
And when kindly falls the night,
In all the town no spark of light.
There I'll come when I'm a man
With a camel caravan;
Light a fire in the gloom
Of some dusty dining room;
See the pictures on the walls,
Heroes, fights, and festivals;
And in a corner find the toys
Of the old Egyptian boys.

A GOOD PLAY

We built a ship upon the stairs
All made of the back-bedroom chairs,
And filled it full of sofa pillows
To go a-sailing on the billows.

We took a saw and several nails,
And water in the nursery pails;
And Tom said, "Let us also take
An apple and a slice of cake" —
Which was enough for Tom and me
To go a-sailing on, till tea.

We sailed along for days and days
And had the very best of plays;
But Tom fell out and hurt his knee,
So there was no one left but me.

SINGING

Of speckled eggs the birdie sings
   And nests among the trees;
The sailor sings of ropes and things
   In ships upon the seas.

The children sing in far Japan,
   The children sing in Spain;
The organ with the organ man
   Is singing in the rain.

LOOKING FORWARD

When I am grown to man's estate
I shall be very proud and great,
And tell the other girls and boys
Not to meddle with my toys.

THE LAND OF COUNTERPANE

When I was sick and lay abed,
I had two pillows at my head,
And all my toys beside me lay
To keep me happy all the day.

And sometimes for an hour or so
I watched my leaden soldiers go,
With different uniforms and drills,
Among the bedclothes, through the hills;

And sometimes sent my ships in fleets
All up and down among the sheets;
Or brought my trees and houses out,
And planted cities all about.

I was the giant great and still
That sits upon the pillow hill,
And sees before him, dale and plain,
The pleasant land of counterpane.

MY SHADOW

I have a little shadow that goes in and out with me,
And what can be the use of him is more than I can see.
He is very, very like me from the heels up to the head;
And I see him jump before me, when I jump into my bed.

The funniest thing about him is the way he likes to grow —
Not at all like proper children, which is always very slow;
For he sometimes shoots up taller like an india-rubber ball,
And he sometimes gets so little that there's none of him at all.

He hasn't got a notion of how children ought to play,
And can only make a fool of me in every sort of way.
He stays so close beside me, he's a coward you can see;
I'd think shame to stick to nursie as that shadow sticks to me!

One morning, very early, before the sun was up,
I rose and found the shining dew on every buttercup;
But my lazy little shadow, like an arrant sleepyhead,
Had stayed at home behind me and was fast asleep in bed.

WHERE GO THE BOATS?

Dark brown is the river,
   Golden is the sand.
It flows along forever,
   With trees on either hand.

Green leaves a-floating,
   Castles of the foam,
Boats of mine a-boating—
   Where will all come home?

On goes the river
   And out past the mill,
Away down the valley,
   Away down the hill.

Away down the river,
   A hundred miles or more,
Other little children
   Shall bring my boats ashore.

AUNTIE'S SKIRTS

Whenever Auntie moves around,
Her dresses make a curious sound,
They trail behind her up the floor,
And trundle after through the door.

SYSTEM

Every night my prayers I say,
And get my dinner every day;
And every day that I've been good,
I get an orange after food.

The child that is not clean and neat,
With lots of toys and things to eat,
He is a naughty child, I'm sure—
Or else his dear papa is poor.

A Good Boy

I woke before the morning, I was happy all the day,
I never said an ugly word, but smiled and stuck to play.

And now at last the sun is going down behind the wood,
And I am very happy, for I know that I've been good.

My bed is waiting cool and fresh, with linen smooth and fair
And I must be off to sleepsin-by, and not forget my prayer.

I know that, till tomorrow I shall see the sun arise,
No ugly dream shall fright my mind, no ugly sight my eyes.

But slumber hold me tightly till I waken in the dawn,
And hear the thrushes singing in the lilacs round the lawn.

THE LAND OF NOD

From breakfast on through all the day
At home among my friends I stay,
But every night I go abroad
Afar into the land of Nod.

All by myself I have to go,
With none to tell me what to do—
All alone beside the streams
And up the mountainsides of dreams.

The strangest things are there for me,
Both things to eat and things to see,
And many frightening sights abroad
Till morning in the land of Nod.

Try as I like to find the way,
I never can get back by day,
Nor can remember plain and clear
The curious music that I hear.

MARCHING SONG

Bring the comb and play upon it!
  Marching, here we come!
Willie cocks his highland bonnet,
  Johnnie beats the drum.

Mary Jane commands the party,
  Peter leads the rear;
Feet in time, alert and hearty,
  Each a grenadier!

All in the most martial manner
    Marching double-quick;
While the napkin, like a banner,
    Waves upon the stick!

Here's enough of fame and pillage,
    Great commander Jane!
Now that we've been round the village,
    Let's go home again.

ESCAPE AT BEDTIME

The lights from the parlor and kitchen shone out
    Through the blinds and the windows and bars;
And high overhead and all moving about,
    There were thousands of millions of stars.
There ne'er were such thousands of leaves on a tree,
    Nor of people in church or the park,
As the crowds of the stars that looked down upon me,
    And that glittered and winked in the dark.

The Dog, and the Plow, and the Hunter, and all,
    And the star of the sailor, and Mars,
These shone in the sky, and the pail by the wall
    Would be half full of water and stars.

They saw me at last, and they chased me with cries,
    And they soon had me packed into bed;
But the glory kept shining and bright in my eyes,
    And the stars going round in my head.

THE COW

The friendly cow all red and white,
    I love with all my heart:
She gives me cream with all her might,
    To eat with apple tart.

She wanders lowing here and there,
    And yet she cannot stray,
All in the pleasant open air,
    The pleasant light of day;

And blown by all the winds that pass
    And wet with all the showers,
She walks among the meadow grass
    And eats the meadow flowers.

HAPPY THOUGHT

The world is so full of a number of things,
I'm sure we should all be as happy as kings.

THE WIND

I saw you toss the kites on high
And blow the birds about the sky;
And all around I heard you pass,
Like ladies' skirts across the grass—
    O wind, a-blowing all day long,
    O wind, that sings so loud a song!

I saw the different things you did,
But always you yourself you hid.
I felt you push, I heard you call,
I could not see yourself at all—
    O wind, a-blowing all day long,
    O wind, that sings so loud a song!

O you that are so strong and cold,
O blower, are you young or old?
Are you a beast of field and tree,
Or just a stronger child than me?
    O wind, a-blowing all day long,
    O wind, that sings so loud a song!

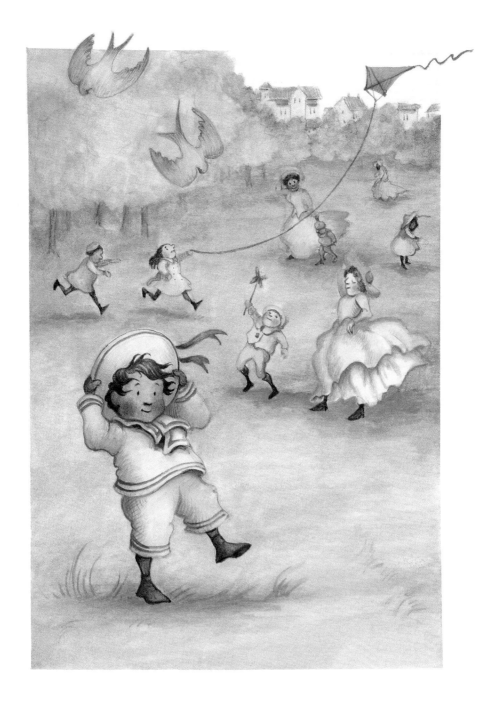

KEEPSAKE MILL

Over the borders, a sin without pardon,
    Breaking the branches and crawling below,
Out through the breach in the wall of the garden,
    Down by the banks of the river we go.

Here is the mill with the humming of thunder,
    Here is the weir with the wonder of foam,
Here is the sluice with the race running under—
    Marvelous places, though handy to home!

Sounds of the village grow stiller and stiller,
    Stiller the note of the birds on the hill;
Dusty and dim are the eyes of the miller,
    Deaf are his ears with the moil of the mill.

Years may go by, and the wheel in the river
   Wheel as it wheels for us, children, today,
Wheel and keep roaring and foaming forever
   Long after all of the boys are away.

Home from the Indies and home from the ocean,
   Heroes and soldiers we all shall come home;
Still we shall find the old mill wheel in motion,
   Turning and churning that river to foam.

You with the bean that I gave when we quarreled,
   I with your marble of Saturday last,
Honored and old and all gaily appareled,
   Here we shall meet and remember the past.

GOOD AND BAD CHILDREN

Children, you are very little,
And your bones are very brittle;
If you would grow great and stately,
You must try to walk sedately.

You must still be bright and quiet,
And content with simple diet;
And remain, through all bewild'ring,
Innocent and honest children.

Happy hearts and happy faces,
Happy play in grassy places—
That was how, in ancient ages,
Children grew to kings and sages.

But the unkind and the unruly,
And the sort who eat unduly,
They must never hope for glory—
Theirs is quite a different story!

Cruel children, crying babies,
All grow up as geese and gabies,
Hated, as their age increases,
By their nephews and their nieces.

FOREIGN CHILDREN

Little Indian, Sioux or Crow,
Little frosty Eskimo,
Little Turk or Japanee,
Oh! Don't you wish that you were me?

You have seen the scarlet trees
And the lions over seas;
You have eaten ostrich eggs,
And turned the turtles off their legs.

Such a life is very fine,
But it's not so nice as mine:
You must often, as you trod,
Have wearied *not* to be abroad.

You have curious things to eat,
I am fed on proper meat;
You must dwell beyond the foam,
But I am safe and live at home.
    Little Indian, Sioux or Crow,
    Little frosty Eskimo,
    Little Turk or Japanee,
Oh! Don't you wish that you were me?

FOREIGN LANDS

Up into the cherry tree
Who should climb but little me?
I held the trunk with both my hands
And looked abroad on foreign lands.

I saw the next-door garden lie,
Adorned with flowers, before my eye,
And many pleasant places more
That I had never seen before.

I saw the dimpling river pass
And be the sky's blue looking glass;
The dusty roads go up and down
With people tramping into town.

If I could find a higher tree
Farther and farther I should see,
To where the grown-up river slips
Into the sea among the ships,

To where the roads on either hand
Lead onward into fairy land,
Where all the children dine at five,
And all the playthings come alive.

THE LAMPLIGHTER

My tea is nearly ready and the sun has left the sky.
It's time to take the window to see Leerie going by;
For every night at teatime and before you take your seat,
With lantern and with ladder he comes posting up the street.

Now Tom would be a driver and Maria go to sea,
And my papa's a banker and as rich as he can be;
But I, when I am stronger and can choose what I'm to do,
O Leerie, I'll go round at night and light the lamps with you!

For we are very lucky, with a lamp before the door,
And Leerie stops to light it as he lights so many more;
And oh! Before you hurry by with ladder and with light;
O Leerie, see a little child and nod to him tonight!

MY BED IS A BOAT

My bed is like a little boat;
    Nurse helps me in when I embark;
She girds me in my sailor's coat
    And starts me in the dark.

At night, I go on board and say
    Good night to all my friends on shore;
I shut my eyes and sail away
    And see and hear no more.

And sometimes things to bed I take,
    As prudent sailors have to do;
Perhaps a slice of wedding cake,
    Perhaps a toy or two.

All night across the dark we steer;
    But when the day returns at last,
Safe in my room, beside the pier,
    I find my vessel fast.

THE MOON

The moon has a face like the clock in the hall;
She shines on thieves on the garden wall,
On streets and field and harbor quays,
And birdies asleep in the forks of the trees.

The squalling cat and the squeaking mouse,
The howling dog by the door of the house,
The bat that lies in bed at noon,
All love to be out by the light of the moon.

But all of the things that belong to the day
Cuddle to sleep to be out of her way;
And flowers and children close their eyes
Till up in the morning the sun shall arise.

THE SWING

How do you like to go up in a swing,
    Up in the air so blue?
Oh, I do think it the pleasantest thing
    Ever a child can do!

Up in the air and over the wall,
    Till I can see so wide,
Rivers and trees and cattle and all
    Over the countryside—

Till I look down on the garden green,
    Down on the roof so brown—
Up in the air I go flying again,
    Up in the air and down!

LOOKING-GLASS RIVER

Smooth it glides upon its travel,
   Here a wimple, there a gleam—
     O the clean gravel!
     O the smooth stream!

Sailing blossoms, silver fishes,
   Paven pools as clear as air—
     How a child wishes
     To live down there!

We can see our colored faces
   Floating on the shaken pool
     Down in cool places,
     Dim and very cool;

Till a wind or water wrinkle,
    Dipping marten, plumping trout,
      Spreads in a twinkle
      And blots all out.

See the rings pursue each other;
    All below grows black as night,
      Just as if mother
      Had blown out the light!

Patience, children, just a minute—
    See the spreading circles die;
      The stream and all in it
      Will clear by-and-by.

THE HAYLOFT

Through all the pleasant meadowside
    The grass grew shoulder high,
Till the shining scythes went far and wide
    And cut it down to dry.

Those green and sweetly smelling crops
    They led in wagons home;
And they piled them here in mountaintops
    For mountaineers to roam.

Here is Mount Clear, Mount Rusty Nail,
    Mount Eagle and Mount High—
The mice that in these mountains dwell,
    No happier are than I!

Oh, what a joy to clamber there,
    Oh, what a place for play,
With the sweet, the dim, the dusty air,
    The happy hills of hay!

FROM A RAILWAY CARRIAGE

Faster than fairies, faster than witches,
Bridges and houses, hedges and ditches;
And charging along like troops in a battle
All through the meadows the horses and cattle:
All of the sights of the hill and the plain
Fly as thick as driving rain;
And ever again, in the wink of an eye,
Painted stations whistle by.
Here is a child who clambers and scrambles,
All by himself and gathering brambles;
Here is a tramp who stands and gazes;
And there is the green for stringing the daisies!
Here is a cart run away in the road
Lumping along with man and load;
And here is a mill, and there is a river:
Each a glimpse and gone forever!

FAIRY BREAD

Come up here, O dusty feet!
    Here is fairy bread to eat.
Here in my retiring room,
    Children, you may dine
On the golden smell of broom
    And the shade of pine;
And when you have eaten well,
Fairy stories hear and tell.

WINTERTIME

Late lies the wintry sun abed,
A frosty, fiery sleepyhead;
Blinks but an hour or two; and then,
A bloodred orange, sets again.

Before the stars have left the skies,
At morning in the dark I rise;
And shivering in my nakedness,
By the cold candle, bathe and dress.

Close by the jolly fire I sit
To warm my frozen bones a bit;
Or with a reindeer sled, explore
The colder countries round the door.

When to go out, my nurse doth wrap
Me in my comforter and cap;
The cold wind burns my face, and blows
Its frosty pepper up my nose.

Black are my steps on silver sod;
Thick blows my frosty breath abroad;
And tree and house, and hill and lake,
Are frosted like a wedding cake.

TIME TO RISE

A birdie with a yellow bill
Hopped upon the windowsill,
Cocked his shining eye and said:
"Ain't you 'shamed, you sleepyhead!"

FAREWELL TO THE FARM

The coach is at the door at last;
The eager children, mounting fast
And kissing hands, in chorus sing:
Good-bye, good-bye, to everything!

To house and garden, field and lawn,
The meadow gates we swang upon,
To pump and stable, tree and swing,
Good-bye, good-bye, to everything!

And fare you well forevermore,
O ladder at the hayloft door,
O hayloft where the cobwebs cling,
Good-bye, good-bye, to everything!

Crack goes the whip, and off we go;
The trees and houses smaller grow;
Last, round the woody turn we swing:
Good-bye, good-bye, to everything!

NORTHWEST PASSAGE

1. Good Night

When the bright lamp is carried in,
The sunless hours again begin;
O'er all without, in field and lane,
The haunted night returns again.

Now we behold the embers flee
About the firelit hearth; and see
Our faces painted as we pass,
Like pictures, on the window glass.

Must we to bed indeed? Well then,
Let us arise and go like men,
And face with an undaunted tread
The long black passage up to bed.

Farewell, O brother, sister, sire!
O pleasant party round the fire!
The songs you sing, the tales you tell,
Till far tomorrow, fare ye well!

2. Shadow March

All round the house is the jet black night;
  It stares through the windowpane;
It crawls in the corners, hiding from the light,
  And it moves with the moving flame.

Now my little heart goes a-beating like a drum,
  With the breath of the Bogie in my hair;
And all round the candle the crooked shadows come,
  And go marching along up the stair.

The shadow of the balusters, the shadow of the lamp,
  The shadow of the child that goes to bed—
All the wicked shadows coming, tramp, tramp, tramp,
  With the black night overhead.

3. In Port

Last, to the chamber where I lie
My fearful footsteps patter nigh,
And come from out the cold and gloom
Into my warm and cheerful room.

There, safe arrived, we turn about
To keep the coming shadows out,
And close the happy door at last
On all the perils that we passed.

Then, when Mama goes by to bed,
She shall come in with tiptoe tread,
And see me lying warm and fast
And in the land of Nod at last.

The Child Alone

THE UNSEEN PLAYMATE

When children are playing alone on the green,
In comes the playmate that never was seen.
When children are happy and lonely and good,
The Friend of the Children comes out of the wood.

Nobody heard him and nobody saw,
His is a picture you never could draw,
But he's sure to be present, abroad or at home,
When children are happy and playing alone.

He lies in the laurels, he runs on the grass,
He sings when you tinkle the musical glass;
Whene'er you are happy and cannot tell why,
The Friend of the Children is sure to be by!

He loves to be little, he hates to be big,
'Tis he that inhabits the caves that you dig;
'Tis he when you play with your soldiers of tin
That sides with the Frenchmen and never can win.

'Tis he, when at night you go off to your bed,
Bids you go to your sleep and not trouble your head;
For wherever they're lying, in cupboard or shelf,
'Tis he will take care of your playthings himself!

MY SHIP AND I

O it's I that am the captain of a tidy little ship,
    Of a ship that goes a-sailing on the pond;
And my ship it keeps a-turning all around and all about;
But when I'm a little older, I shall find the secret out
    How to send my vessel sailing on beyond.

For I mean to grow as little as the dolly at the helm,
    And the dolly I intend to come alive;
And with him beside to help me, it's a-sailing I shall go,
It's a-sailing on the water, when the jolly breezes blow
    And the vessel goes a divie-divie-dive.

O it's then you'll see me sailing through the rushes and the reeds,
    And you'll hear the water singing at the prow;
For beside the dolly sailor, I'm to voyage and explore,
To land upon the island where no dolly was before,
    And to fire the penny cannon in the bow.

MY KINGDOM

Down by a shining water well
I found a very little dell,
   No higher than my head.
The heather and the gorse about
In summer bloom were coming out,
   Some yellow and some red.

I called the little pool a sea;
The little hills were big to me;
   For I am very small.
I made a boat, I made a town,
I searched the caverns up and down,
   And named them one and all.

And all about was mine, I said,
The little sparrows overhead,
   The little minnows too.
This was the world and I was king;
For me the bees came by to sing,
   For me the swallows flew.

I played there were no deeper seas,
Nor any wider plains than these,
    Nor other kings than me.
At last I heard my mother call
Out from the house at evenfall,
    To call me home to tea.

And I must rise and leave my dell,
And leave my dimpled water well,
    And leave my heather blooms.
Alas! And as my home I neared,
How very big my nurse appeared.
    How great and cool the rooms!

BLOCK CITY

What are you able to build with your blocks?
Castles and palaces, temples and docks.
Rain may keep raining, and others go roam,
But I can be happy and building at home.

Let the sofa be mountains, the carpet be sea,
There I'll establish a city for me:
A kirk and a mill and a palace beside,
And a harbor as well where my vessels may ride.

Great is the palace with pillar and wall,
A sort of a tower on the top of it all,
And steps coming down in an orderly way
To where my toy vessels lie safe in the bay.

This one is sailing and that one is moored:
Hark to the song of the sailors on board!
And see, on the steps of my palace, the kings
Coming and going with presents and things!

Now I have done with it, down let it go!
All in a moment the town is laid low.
Block upon block lying scattered and free,
What is there left of my town by the sea?

Yet as I saw it, I see it again,
The kirk and the palace, the ships and the men,
And as long as I live and where'er I may be,
I'll always remember my town by the sea.

MY TREASURES

These nuts, that I keep in the back of the nest
Where all my lead soldiers are lying at rest,
Were gathered in autumn by nursie and me
In a wood with a well by the side of the sea.

This whistle we made (and how clearly it sounds!)
By the side of a field at the end of the grounds.
Of a branch of a plane, with a knife of my own,
It was nursie who made it, and nursie alone!

The stone, with the white and the yellow and gray,
We discovered I cannot tell *how* far away;
And I carried it back although weary and cold,
For though Father denies it, I'm sure it is gold.

But of all my treasures the last is the king,
For there's very few children possess such a thing;
And that is a chisel, both handle and blade,
Which a man who was really a carpenter made.

PICTURE BOOKS IN WINTER

Summer fading, winter comes —
Frosty mornings, tingling thumbs,
Window robins, winter rooks,
And the picture storybooks.

Water now is turned to stone
Nurse and I can walk upon;
Still we find the flowing brooks
In the picture storybooks.

All the pretty things put by,
Wait upon the children's eye,
Sheep and shepherds, trees and crooks,
In the picture storybooks.

We may see how all things are,
Seas and cities, near and far,
And the flying fairies' looks,
In the picture storybooks.

How am I to sing your praise,
Happy chimney-corner days,
Sitting safe in nursery nooks,
Reading picture storybooks?

ARMIES IN THE FIRE

The lamps now glitter down the street;
Faintly sound the falling feet;
And the blue even slowly falls
About the garden trees and walls.

Now in the falling of the gloom
The red fire paints the empty room:
And warmly on the roof it looks,
And flickers on the backs of books.

Armies march by tower and spire
Of cities blazing, in the fire —
Till as I gaze with staring eyes,
The armies fade, the luster dies.

Then once again the glow returns;
Again the phantom city burns;
And down the red-hot valley, lo!
The phantom armies marching go!

Blinking embers, tell me true
Where are those armies marching to,
And what the burning city is
That crumbles in your furnaces!

THE LAND OF STORYBOOKS

At evening when the lamp is lit,
Around the fire my parents sit;
They sit at home and talk and sing,
And do not play at anything.

Now, with my little gun, I crawl
All in the dark along the wall,
And follow round the forest track
Away behind the sofa back.

There, in the night, where none can spy,
All in my hunter's camp I lie,
And play at books that I have read
Till it is time to go to bed.

These are the hills, these are the woods,
These are my starry solitudes;
And there the river by whose brink
The roaring lions come to drink.

I see the others far away
As if in firelit camp they lay,
And I, like to an Indian scout,
Around their party prowled about.

So, when my nurse comes in for me,
Home I return across the sea,
And go to bed with backward looks
At my dear land of storybooks.

THE LITTLE LAND

When at home alone I sit,
And am very tired of it,
I have just to shut my eyes
To go sailing through the skies—
To go sailing far away
To the pleasant Land of Play;
To the fairy land afar
Where the Little People are;
Where the clover tops are trees,
And the rain pools are the seas,
And the leaves, like little ships,
Sail about on tiny trips;
And above the daisy tree
    Through the grasses,
High o'erhead the Bumble Bee
    Hums and passes.

In that forest to and fro
I can wander, I can go;
See the spider and the fly,
And the ants go marching by,
Carrying parcels with their feet
Down the green and grassy street.
I can in the sorrel sit
Where the ladybird alit.

I can climb the jointed grass
    And on high
See the greater swallows pass
    In the sky,
And the round sun rolling by
Heeding no such things as I.

Through that forest I can pass
Till, as in a looking glass,
Humming fly and daisy tree
And my tiny self I see,
Painted very clear and neat
On the rain pool at my feet.
Should a leaflet come to land
Drifting near to where I stand,
Straight I'll board that tiny boat
Round the rain pool sea to float.

Little thoughtful creatures sit
On the grassy coasts of it;
Little things with lovely eyes
See me sailing with surprise.
Some are clad in armor green—
(These have sure to battle been!)—
Some are pied with ev'ry hue,
Black and crimson, gold and blue;
Some have wings and swift are gone—
But they all look kindly on.

 When my eyes I once again
 Open, and see all things plain:
High bare walls, great bare floor;
Great big knobs on drawer and door;
Great big people perched on chairs,
Stitching tucks and mending tears,
Each a hill that I could climb,
And talking nonsense all the time—
 O dear me,
 That I could be
A sailor on the rain pool sea,
A climber in the clover tree,
And just come back, a sleepyhead,
Late at night to go to bed.

Garden Days

NIGHT AND DAY

When the golden day is done,
   Through the closing portal,
Child and garden, flower and sun,
   Vanish all things mortal.

As the blinding shadows fall
   As the rays diminish,
Under evening's cloak, they all
   Roll away and vanish.

Garden darkened, daisy shut,
   Child in bed, they slumber—
Glowworm in the highway rut,
   Mice among the lumber.

In the darkness houses shine,
   Parents move with candles;
Till on all, the night divine
   Turns the bedroom handles.

Till at last the day begins
   In the east a-breaking,
In the hedges and the whins
   Sleeping birds a-waking.

In the darkness shapes of things,
    Houses, trees and hedges,
Clearer grow; and sparrow's wings
    Beat on window ledges.

These shall wake the yawning maid;
    She the door shall open —
Finding dew on garden glade
    And the morning broken.

There my garden grows again
    Green and rosy painted,
As at eve behind the pane
    From my eyes it fainted.

Just as it was shut away,
    Toylike, in the even,
Here I see it glow with day
    Under glowing heaven.

Every path and every plot,
    Every bush of roses,
Every blue forget-me-not
    Where the dew reposes.

"Up!" they cry. "The day is come
    On the smiling valleys:
We have beat the morning drum;
    Playmate, join your allies!"

NEST EGGS

Birds all the sunny day
    Flutter and quarrel
Here in the arborlike
    Tent of the laurel.

Here in the fork
    The brown nest is seated;
Four little blue eggs
    The mother keeps heated.

While we stand watching her
    Staring like gabies,
Safe in each egg are the
    Bird's little babies.

Soon the frail eggs they shall
    Chip, and upspringing
Make all the April woods
    Merry with singing.

Younger than we are,
　　O children, and frailer,
Soon in blue air they'll be,
　　Singer and sailor.

We, so much older,
　　Taller and stronger,
We shall look down on the
　　Birdies no longer.

They shall go flying
　　With musical speeches
High overhead in the
　　Tops of the beeches.

In spite of our wisdom
　　And sensible talking,
We on our feet must go
　　Plodding and walking.

THE FLOWERS

All the names I know from nurse:
Gardener's garters, Shepherd's purse,
Bachelor's buttons, Lady's smock,
And the Lady Hollyhock.

Fairy places, fairy things,
Fairy woods where the wild bee wings,
Tiny trees for tiny dames—
These must all be fairy names!

Tiny woods below whose boughs
Shady fairies weave a house;
Tiny treetops, rose or thyme,
Where the braver fairies climb!

Fair are grown-up people's trees,
But the fairest woods are these;
Where, if I were not so tall,
I should live for good and all.

THE DUMB SOLDIER

When the grass was closely mown,
Walking on the lawn alone,
In the turf a hole I found,
And hid a soldier underground.

Spring and daisies came apace;
Grasses hide my hiding place;
Grasses run like a green sea
O'er the lawn up to my knee.

Under grass alone he lies,
Looking up with leaden eyes,
Scarlet coat and pointed gun,
To the stars and to the sun.

When the grass is ripe like grain,
When the scythe is stoned again,
When the lawn is shaven clear,
Then my hole shall reappear.

I shall find him, never fear,
I shall find my grenadier;
But for all that's gone and come,
I shall find my soldier dumb.

He has lived, a little thing,
In the grassy woods of spring;
Done, if he could tell me true,
Just as I should like to do.

He has seen the starry hours
And the springing of the flowers;
And the fairy things that pass
In the forests of the grass.

In the silence he has heard
Talking bee and ladybird,
And the butterfly has flown
O'er him as he lay alone.

Not a word will he disclose,
Not a word of all he knows.
I must lay him on the shelf,
And make up the tale myself.

THE GARDENER

The gardener does not love to talk,
He makes me keep the gravel walk;
And when he puts his tools away,
He locks the door and takes the key.

Away behind the currant row,
Where no one else but cook may go,
Far in the plots, I see him dig,
Old and serious, brown and big.

He digs the flowers, green, red, and blue,
Nor wishes to be spoken to.
He digs the flowers and cuts the hay,
And never seems to want to play.

Silly gardener! Summer goes,
And winter comes with pinching toes,
When in the garden bare and brown
You must lay your barrow down.

Well now, and while the summer stays,
To profit by these garden days
O how much wiser you would be
To play at Indian wars with me!

SUMMER SUN

Great is the sun, and wide he goes
Through empty heaven without repose;
And in the blue and glowing days
More thick than rain he showers his rays.

Though closer still the blinds we pull
To keep the shady parlor cool,
Yet he will find a chink or two
To slip his golden fingers through.

The dusty attic spider-clad
He, through the keyhole, maketh glad;
And through the broken edge of tiles
Into the laddered hayloft smiles.

Meantime his golden face around
He bares to all the garden ground,
And sheds a warm and glittering look
Among the ivy's inmost nook.

Above the hills, along the blue,
Round the bright air with footing true,
To please the child, to paint the rose,
The gardener of the world, he goes.

AUTUMN FIRES

In the other gardens
    And all up the vale,
From the autumn bonfires
    See the smoke trail!

Pleasant summer over
    And all the summer flowers,
The red fire blazes,
    The gray smoke towers.

Sing a song of seasons!
    Something bright in all!
Flowers in the summer,
    Fires in the fall!

HISTORICAL ASSOCIATIONS

Dear Uncle Jim, this garden ground
That now you smoke your pipe around,
Has seen immortal actions done
And valiant battles lost and won.

Here we had best on tiptoe tread,
While I for safety march ahead,
For this is that enchanted ground
Where all who loiter slumber sound.

Here is the sea, here is the sand,
Here is simple Shepherd's Land,
Here are the fairy hollyhocks,
And there are Ali Baba's rocks.

But yonder, see! Apart and high,
Frozen Siberia lies; where I,
With Robert Bruce and William Tell,
Was bound by an enchanter's spell.

There, then, a while in chains we lay,
In wintry dungeons, far from day;
But ris'n length, with might and main,
Our iron fetters burst in twain,

Then all the horns were blown in town;
And, to the ramparts clanging down,
All the giants leaped to horse
And charged behind us through the gorse.

On we rode, the others and I,
Over the mountains blue, and by
The Silent River, the sounding sea,
And the robber woods of Tartary.

A thousand miles we galloped fast,
And down the witches' lane we passed,
And rode amain, with brandished sword,
Up to the middle, through the ford.

Last we drew rein — a weary three —
Upon the lawn, in time for tea,
And from our steeds alighted down
Before the gates of Babylon.

Envoys

To Willie and Henrietta

If two may read aright
These rhymes of old delight
And house and garden play,
You too, my cousins, and you only, may.

You in a garden green
With me were king and queen,
Were hunter, soldier, tar,
And all the thousand things that children are.

Now in the elders' seat
We rest with quiet feet,
And from the window bay
We watch the children, our successors, play.

"Time was," the golden head
Irrevocably said;
But time which none can bind,
While flowing fast away, leaves love behind.

TO MY MOTHER

You too, my mother, read my rhymes
For love of unforgotten times,
And you may chance to hear once more
The little feet along the floor.

TO AUNTIE

Chief of our aunts — not only I,
But all your dozen of nurselings cry —
What did the other children do?
And what were childhood, wanting you?

TO MINNIE

The red room with the giant bed
Where none but elders laid their head;
The little room where you and I
Did for awhile together lie
And, simple suitor, I your hand
In decent marriage did demand;
The great day nursery, best of all,
With pictures pasted on the wall
And leaves upon the blind
A pleasant room wherein to wake
And hear the leafy garden shake
And rustle in the wind —
And pleasant there to lie in bed
And see the pictures overhead —
The wars about Sebastopol,
The grinning guns along the wall,
The daring escalade,
The plunging ships, the bleating sheep,
The happy children ankle-deep
And laughing as they wade;

All these are vanished clean away,
And the old manse is changed today;
It wears an altered face
And shields a stranger race.
The river, on from mill to mill,
Flows past our childhood's garden still;
But ah! We children nevermore
Shall watch it from the water door.
Below the yew—it still is there—
Our phantom voices haunt the air
As we were still at play,
And I can hear them call and say:
"How far is it to Babylon?"

Ah, far enough, my dear,
Far, far enough from here —
Yet you have farther gone!
"Can I get there by candlelight?"
So goes the old refrain.
I do not know — perchance you might —
But only, children, hear it right,
Ah, never to return again!
The eternal dawn, beyond a doubt,
Shall break on hill and plain,
And put all stars and candles out
Ere we be young again.

To you in distant India, these
I send across the seas,
Nor count it far across.
For which of us forgets
The Indian cabinets,
The bones of antelope, the wings of albatross,
The pied and painted birds and beans,
The junks and bangles, beads and screens,
The gods and sacred bells,
And the loud-humming, twisting shells!
The level of the parlor floor
Was honest, homely, Scottish shore;
But when we climbed upon a chair,
Behold the gorgeous East was there!
Be this a fable; and behold
Me in the parlor as of old,
And Minnie just above me set
In the quaint Indian cabinet!
Smiling and kind, you grace a shelf
Too high for me to reach myself.
Reach down a hand, my dear, and take
These rhymes for old acquaintance' sake!

TO MY NAME-CHILD

1

Someday soon this rhyming volume, if you learn with proper speed,
Little Louis Sanchez, will be given you to read.
Then shall you discover, that your name was printed down
By the English printers, long before, in London town.

In the great and busy city where the East and West are met,
All the little letters did the English printer set;
While you thought of nothing, and were still too young to play,
Foreign people thought of you in places far away.

Ay, and while you slept, a baby, over all the English lands
Other little children took the volume in their hands;
Other children questioned, in their homes across the seas:
Who was little Louis, won't you tell us, Mother, please?

2

Now that you have spelt your lesson, lay it down and go and play,
Seeking shells and seaweed on the sands of Monterey,
Watching all the mighty whalebones, lying buried by the breeze,
Tiny sandpipers, and the huge Pacific seas.

And remember in your playing, as the sea fog rolls to you,
Long ere you could read it, how I told you what to do;
And that while you thought of no one, nearly half the world away
Someone thought of Louis on the beach of Monterey!

TO ANY READER

As from the house your mother sees
You playing round the garden trees,
So you may see, if you will look
Through the windows of this book,
Another child, far, far away,
And in another garden, play.
But do not think you can at all,
By knocking on the window, call
That child to hear you. He intent
Is all on his play-business bent.
He does not hear; he will not look,
Nor yet be lured out of this book.
For, long ago, the truth to say,
He has grown up and gone away,
And it is but a child of air
That lingers in the garden there.

Afterword

Robert Louis Stevenson was born in Edinburgh, Scotland, in 1850. Because of his mother's poor health, he was raised mostly by his nurse, Alison Cunningham, to whom he dedicated *A Child's Garden of Verses*. A sickly child himself, Stevenson did not learn to read until he was seven, but he was often soothed through feverish nights by imaginative tales that his father told him.

Stevenson went to school at Edinburgh Academy and at age seventeen entered Edinburgh University. Although he studied civil engineering with the intent of pleasing his father by entering the family firm, he decided when he was twenty-one that what he really wanted to be was a writer. His first book was published in 1878, and over the next sixteen years he produced some of the most popular and beloved books in the history of children's literature, including *Treasure Island*, *Kidnapped*, *The Strange Case of Dr. Jekyll and Mr. Hyde*, and *A Child's Garden of Verses*.

First published in 1885, without any illustrations, *A Child's Garden of Verses* was Stevenson's only major book of poetry for children. By combining his own nostalgic recollections of childhood with his clear understanding of the little boy still inside him, he created a collection of verse that is by turns touching, humorous, plaintive, and joyous. While some of the poems reveal Stevenson's own childhood feelings and experiences, others marvelously capture the world of childhood as seen by adult observers. By combining these two viewpoints, Stevenson created a collection of poems that draws both children and adults to share the verses again and again.

Though many artists have brought their own vision to *A Child's Garden of Verses* in the century since its initial publication, most illustrated editions have been overly sentimental, ignoring the humor and joy expressed in so many of the poems. In this new edition, Caldecott Honor artist Diane Goode has created a suite of more than seventy full-color and black-and-white illustrations that reflect not only the gentle side of these classic verses but also all the exuberance, laughter, and good-natured mischief that are a part of every childhood. By doing so, she has created a lively new edition that is sure to capture the hearts of adults and children today and for many tomorrows to come.

—Peter Glassman

OZ TITLES IN THE
Books of Wonder Series

Tik-Tok of Oz
by L. Frank Baum
with 12 full-color plates and 78 black-and-white illustrations
by John R. Neill

The Scarecrow of Oz
by L. Frank Baum
with 12 full-color plates and 104 black-and-white illustrations
by John R. Neill

Rinkitink in Oz
by L. Frank Baum
with 12 full-color plates and 97 black-and-white illustrations
by John R. Neill

The Lost Princess of Oz
by L. Frank Baum
with 12 full-color plates and 98 black-and-white illustrations
by John R. Neill

Little Wizard Stories of Oz
by L. Frank Baum
with 45 full-color illustrations
by John R. Neill

Dorothy of Oz
by Roger S. Baum
with full-color frontispiece and 50 black-and-white illustrations
by Elizabeth Miles

If you enjoy the Oz books and want to know more about Oz, you may be interested in The Royal Club of Oz. Devoted to America's favorite fairyland, it is a club for everyone who loves the Oz Books. For free information, please send a first-class stamp to:

THE ROYAL CLUB OF OZ
P.O. Box 714
New York, New York 10011
or call toll free: (800) 207-6968

THE THREE MUSKETEERS
by Alexandre Dumas
illustrated by Tom Kidd

THE MAGICAL LAND OF NOOM
written and illustrated by Johnny Gruelle

THE GIFT OF THE MAGI
by O. Henry
illustrated by Michael Dooling

THE LEGEND OF SLEEPY HOLLOW
by Washington Irving
illustrated by Arthur Rackham

RIP VAN WINKLE
by Washington Irving
illustrated by N. C. Wyeth

THE WATER-BABIES
by Charles Kingsley
illustrated by Jessie Willcox Smith

THE JUNGLE BOOK
by Rudyard Kipling
illustrated by Jerry Pinkney

JUST SO STORIES
by Rudyard Kipling
illustrated by Barry Moser

THE RAINBOW FAIRY BOOK
by Andrew Lang
illustrated by Michael Hague

THE STORY OF DOCTOR DOLITTLE
by Hugh Lofting
illustrated by Michael Hague

AT THE BACK OF THE NORTH WIND
by George MacDonald
illustrated by Jessie Willcox Smith

THE PRINCESS AND THE GOBLIN
by George MacDonald
illustrated by Jessie Willcox Smith

GREAT GHOST STORIES
selected and illustrated by Barry Moser

THE ENCHANTED CASTLE
by E. Nesbit
illustrated by Paul O. Zelinsky

TALES OF EDGAR ALLAN POE
by Edgar Allan Poe
illustrated by Barry Moser

BLACK BEAUTY
by Anna Sewell
illustrated by Lucy Kemp-Welch

HEIDI
by Johanna Spyri
illustrated by Jessie Willcox Smith

A CHILD'S GARDEN OF VERSES
by Robert Louis Stevenson
illustrated by Diane Goode

THE ADVENTURES OF HUCKLEBERRY FINN
by Mark Twain
illustrated by Steven Kellogg

THE ADVENTURES OF TOM SAWYER
by Mark Twain
illustrated by Barry Moser

A CONNECTICUT YANKEE IN KING ARTHUR'S COURT
by Mark Twain
illustrated by Trina Schart Hyman

AROUND THE WORLD IN EIGHTY DAYS
by Jules Verne
illustrated by Barry Moser

REBECCA OF SUNNYBROOK FARM
by Kate Douglas Wiggin
illustrated by Helen Mason Grose

THE HAPPY PRINCE AND OTHER STORIES
by Oscar Wilde
illustrated by Charles Robinson